WITHDRAWN

BIG MACHINES

Tractors

David and Penny Glover

Smart Apple Media

J
631.3
GLOVER

HILLS MEMORIAL LIBRARY

MAR 1 3 2006

$18.95

First published in 2004 by Franklin Watts
96 Leonard Street, London EC2A 4XD

Franklin Watts Australia
45-51 Huntley Street, Alexandria, NSW 2015

This edition published under license from Franklin Watts. All rights reserved.
Copyright © 2004 Franklin Watts.

Series editor: Sarah Peutrill, Designer: Richard Langford, Art director: Jonathan Hair
Reading consultant: Margaret Perkins, Institute of Education, University of Reading

Picture credits: Geoff Ashcroft: 4, 20, 23t. Nigel Cattlin/Holt Studios: 15b, 21t. Courtesy of John Deere Ltd:
front cover, 6, 7, 8, 9t, 10, 11b, 12, 13, 14, 15t, 16, 17b, 18, 19t, 23b. Willem Harinck/Holt Studios: 22. Rosie
Jordan/Holt Studios: 19b. Inga Spence/Holt Studios: 21b.

Published in the United States by Smart Apple Media
2140 Howard Drive West, North Mankato, Minnesota 56003

U.S. publication copyright © 2006 Smart Apple Media
International copyright reserved in all countries. No part of this book may be reproduced in any form without
written permission from the publisher.
Printed in the United States of America

Library of Congress Cataloging-in-Publication Data

Glover, David, 1953 Sept. 4-
Tractors / by David and Penny Glover.
p. cm. — (Big machines)
ISBN 1-58340-703-0
1. Tractors—Juvenile literature. I. Glover, Penny. II. Title. III. Series.

TL233.15.G58 2005
631.3'72—dc22   2004052515

2 4 6 8 9 7 5 3

Contents

Tractor work 6

Big wheels 8

The engine 10

Driver's seat 12

Pulling 14

Lifting and loading 16

Sound and light 18

On the road 20

Enormous tractors 22

Make it yourself 24

Trace your own tractor 27

Tractor words 28

Index 30

Tractor work

Tractors are big machines. They can do many different kinds of work. They move soil at building sites, drag logs in forests, and tow trailers on the road.

BIG FACT

There are more than 10 million tractors at work in the world!

This tractor is pulling a trailer.

Tractors can lift as well as pull or push.

Tractors are used mainly on farms. Farmers use them to pull plows and to work other farm machines. Tractors can pull heavy loads over rough ground.

Big wheels

Tractors must cross all kinds of ground. Farmers drive them along muddy tracks, over bumpy fields, and even through shallow water.

BIG FACT

Giant tractor wheels are taller than a grown man!

The tractor's big wheels let it cross sticky mud and rough rocks. Small wheels would sink or get stuck.

Huge tires spread the tractor's weight. They flatten bumps and keep the tractor from sinking into soft ground.

Groove

Axle

Tire

The axle is the rod to which the wheel is attached.

Deep grooves help the tires grip in soft soil. They work like the grips on the bottom of athletic shoes.

The engine

A tractor has a very strong engine to give it the power to move and pull loads.

The engine is at the front of the tractor.

Engine

A big tractor engine has the power of 200 horses!

The engine runs on diesel fuel. The fuel burns inside the engine, making a hot gas that pushes the parts around.

The engine turns gears in the gearbox. These are connected to the driveshaft, which turns the tractor's wheels.

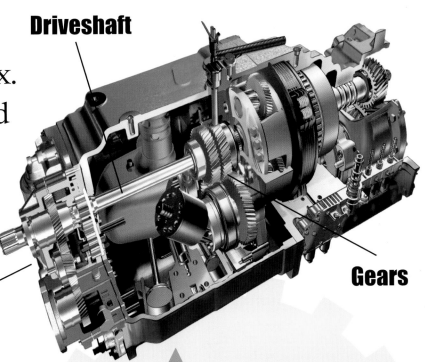

Driveshaft

Gears

Gearbox

▲ Gears are wheels with teeth. They carry the force from the engine through the driveshaft to the big back wheels, just like the gears on a bicycle.

The different machines the tractor pulls, such as a plow, may need power, too. They get this from the tractor's engine.

Driveshaft

A driveshaft turns a grass cutter. ▶

Driver's seat

The tractor driver sits on a seat inside the cab. The cab is very strong. It must keep the driver safe if the tractor accidentally tips over in a ditch or on a steep slope.

The cab is high above the ground, so the driver has a good view.

Control panel   **Steering wheel**

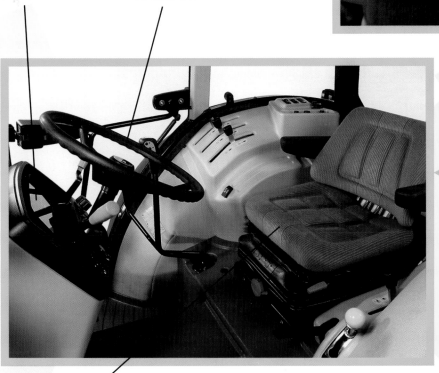

Seat

The seat is soft and comfortable. Farmers sometimes have to sit in tractors all day.

The driver steers the tractor with the steering wheel. The steering wheel turns the front wheels to the right or left to make the tractor turn. Levers, switches, and buttons work all the tractor parts.

Pulling power

A tractor's main job is pulling. That's how it got its name. The word "traction" means pulling power.

The farmer hitches a plow to the back of the tractor. This allows the tractor to pull the plow across the field. Plowing breaks up the soil. The tractor's big wheels keep it from getting stuck as the blades cut into the soil.

BIG FACT

A modern plow can have 12 blades!

Plow

The curved plow blades are called shares. Their special shape turns the soil over, making lines called furrows across the field.

The tractor can lift the blades when all the plowing is done.

Blades (Shares)

Tractor to the rescue! When another vehicle is stuck in the mud, a tractor can pull it free.

Lifting and loading

When hay needs stacking, a tractor can do the job. A lifting arm is attached at the front of the tractor. The farmer drives the tractor forward to pick up the load. Then the farmer moves a lever to lift it into the air.

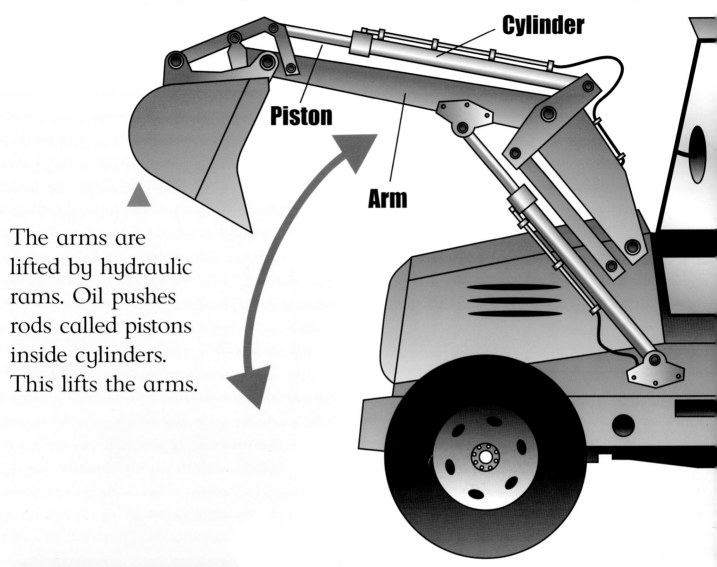

Cylinder

Piston

Arm

The arms are lifted by hydraulic rams. Oil pushes rods called pistons inside cylinders. This lifts the arms.

A tractor can also be fitted with a scoop to lift sand or soil.

Sound and light

A tractor has all the lights a car has—headlights, taillights, brake lights, and turn signals. This means it can travel on the road at any time.

Turn Signals

Spotlights

Headlights

When the crops are ready, there is no time to lose. Tractors are fitted with extra spotlights so the farmer can gather the harvest through the night.

CD player   **Two- way radio**

The driver can keep in touch with other workers on the farm with the two-way radio.

Music from a CD player keeps this driver entertained as he works alone in the fields.

19

On the road

At harvest time, there are a lot of tractors with trailers on the roads. The trailers carry vegetables, fruit, or grain. The farmer takes each load to a barn where it is stored, waiting to be taken to a supermarket or a food factory.

Trailer

A hydraulic
ram tilts the
trailer.

**Hydraulic
ram**

Load

A back gate
is opened,
and the load
pours out.

Enormous tractors

A big tractor can plow faster than a small one. It can pull several machines in "gangs" to plow and level more soil at the same time.

Big tractors are four-wheel drive. This means the engine turns the front wheels as well as the back wheels.

▲ Four-wheel drive and more wheels give the tractor better grip.

A big tractor has twice as many wheels to spread its great weight over the soft ground.

BIG FACT

In tractor-pulling contests, special tractors with huge engines compete to pull the biggest load!

This tractor ▶ has eight wheels.

Make it yourself

Make a box model tractor and trailer.

You will need:

An adult to help

Paints

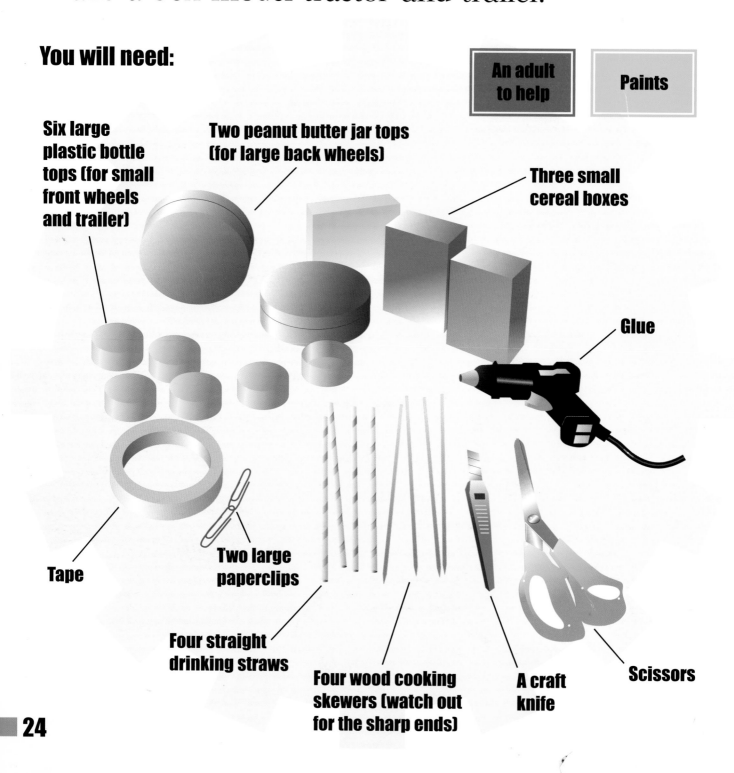

Six large plastic bottle tops (for small front wheels and trailer)

Two peanut butter jar tops (for large back wheels)

Three small cereal boxes

Glue

Tape

Two large paperclips

Four straight drinking straws

Four wood cooking skewers (watch out for the sharp ends)

A craft knife

Scissors

NOTE! Get an adult to help you with the cutting and glueing.

1. Glue two boxes together to make the tractor body and cab.

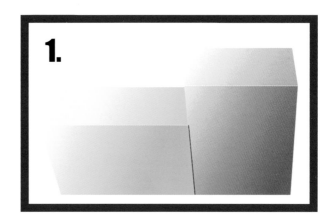

2. Cut the side from one of the cereal boxes to make the trailer body.

Mark and make pairs of holes in the tractor and trailer bodies. Push a straw through each pair of holes. Cut to length.

This straw is a bit higher for the larger back wheel.

3. Slide the skewers through the straws. These are axles.

Make small holes in the centers of the wheels. Push the large wheels onto the axles at the back of the tractor. Glue them in place. Do the same with the small wheels at the front of the tractor and the trailer.

Cut the axles so they do not stick out too far from the wheels.

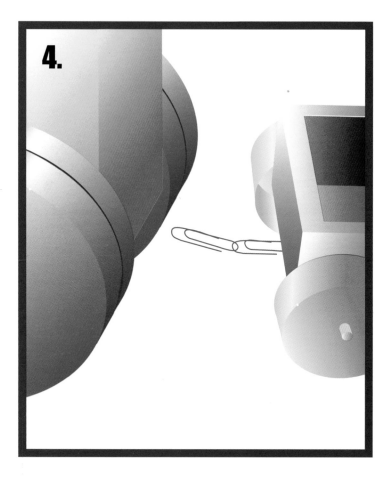

4. Tape or glue one paperclip to the back of the tractor and one to the front of the trailer. This is the hitch.

5. Decorate your model with paint.

Hitch your trailer to your tractor (clip the paperclips together). Test your model on a rough surface. Which roll best, the big tractor wheels or the small ones?

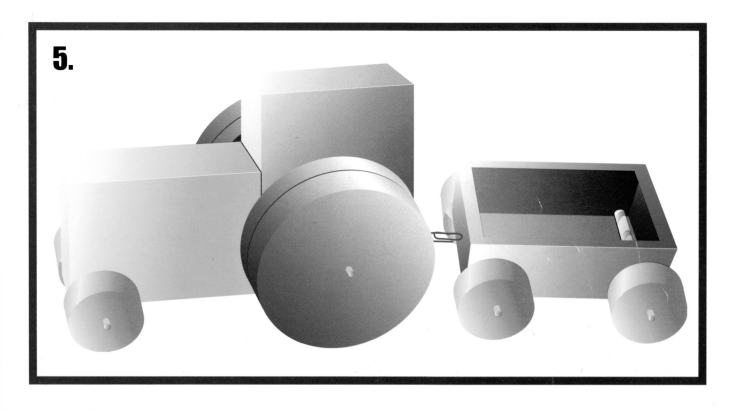

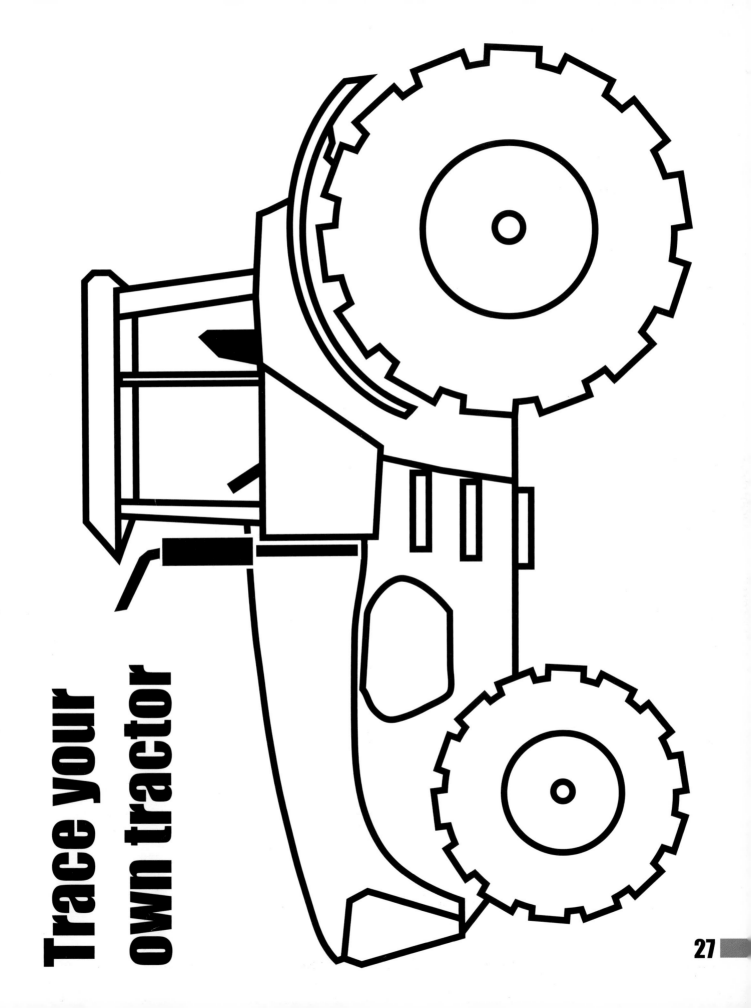

Trace your
own tractor

Tractor words

axle
The rod through the center of a wheel.

cab
The part of a tractor in which the driver sits.

diesel
The fuel a tractor engine uses to make it go.

engine
The part of a machine that burns fuel to make the forces that turn its wheels and move its parts.

four-wheel drive
A tractor or other vehicle in which the engine turns all four wheels.

gear
A wheel with teeth that carries the turning force from the engine to other parts of a machine.

groove
A deep line cut into a wheel.

hydraulic ram

The part on a tractor that pushes to lift a load or tip a trailer. The ram is worked by oil, which pushes a rod called a piston along a cylinder.

load

The things the tractor carries in its trailer, such as vegetables, fruit, or grain.

plow

A farm machine that breaks up the soil in a field when it is pulled behind a tractor.

spotlight

A very bright light that lights up the area at which it is pointed.

tire

The rubber ring filled with air on the outside of a wheel.

trailer

A wagon or truck pulled by a tractor to carry a load.

Index

axle 9, 25, 28

blades (shares) 14, 15

cab 12, 13, 28

diesel 10, 28

engine 10-11, 22, 23, 28

four-wheel drive 22, 28
fuel 10

gear 11, 28
gearbox 11
groove 9, 28

harvest 19, 20
hydraulic ram 17, 21, 28

lever 13, 16
lifting arm 16-17
load 10, 16, 20, 21, 28

piston 17
plow 7, 11, 14, 22, 28
power 10, 11

radio 19

seat 12, 13
spotlight 18, 19, 28
steering wheel 13

tire 9, 28
tractor-pulling contest 23
trailer 6, 20, 21, 24, 25, 26, 28

wheel 8-9, 11, 13, 14, 22, 23, 24, 25